Color Me High

Sugar Skulls

A Marijuana Inspired Adult Coloring Book

Created by Faith Marigold

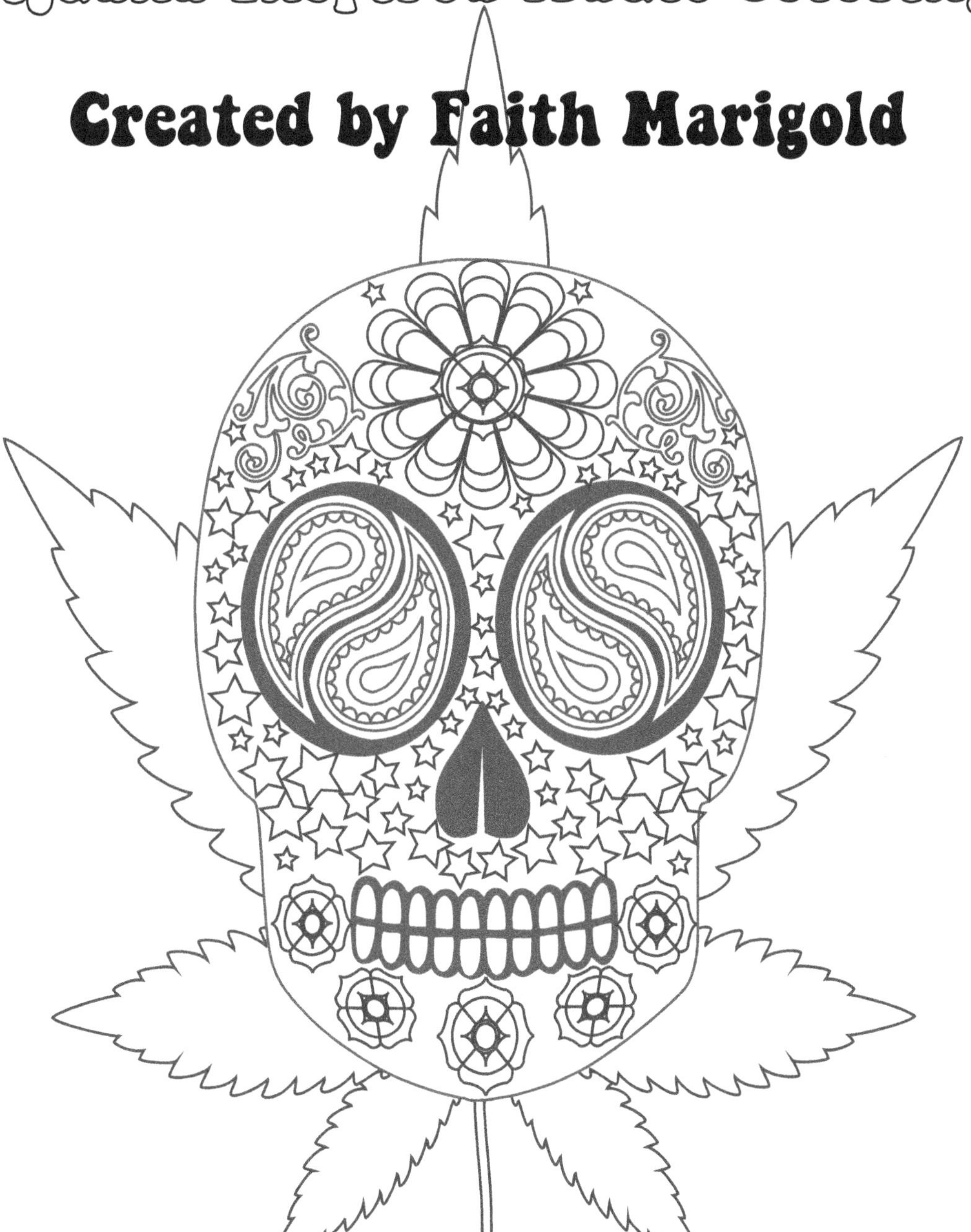

ISBN-13: 978-1530991297
ISBN-10: 1530991293

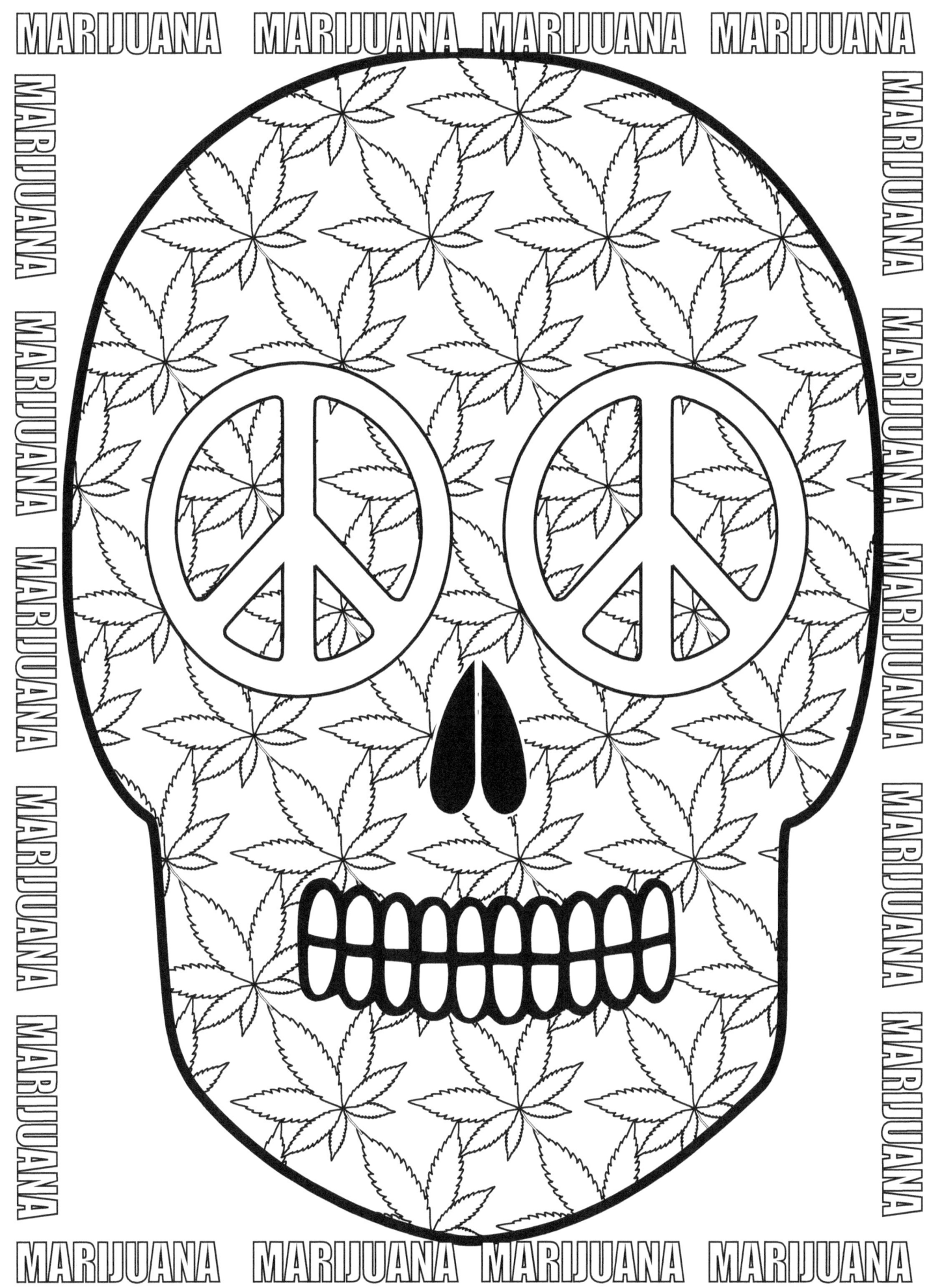

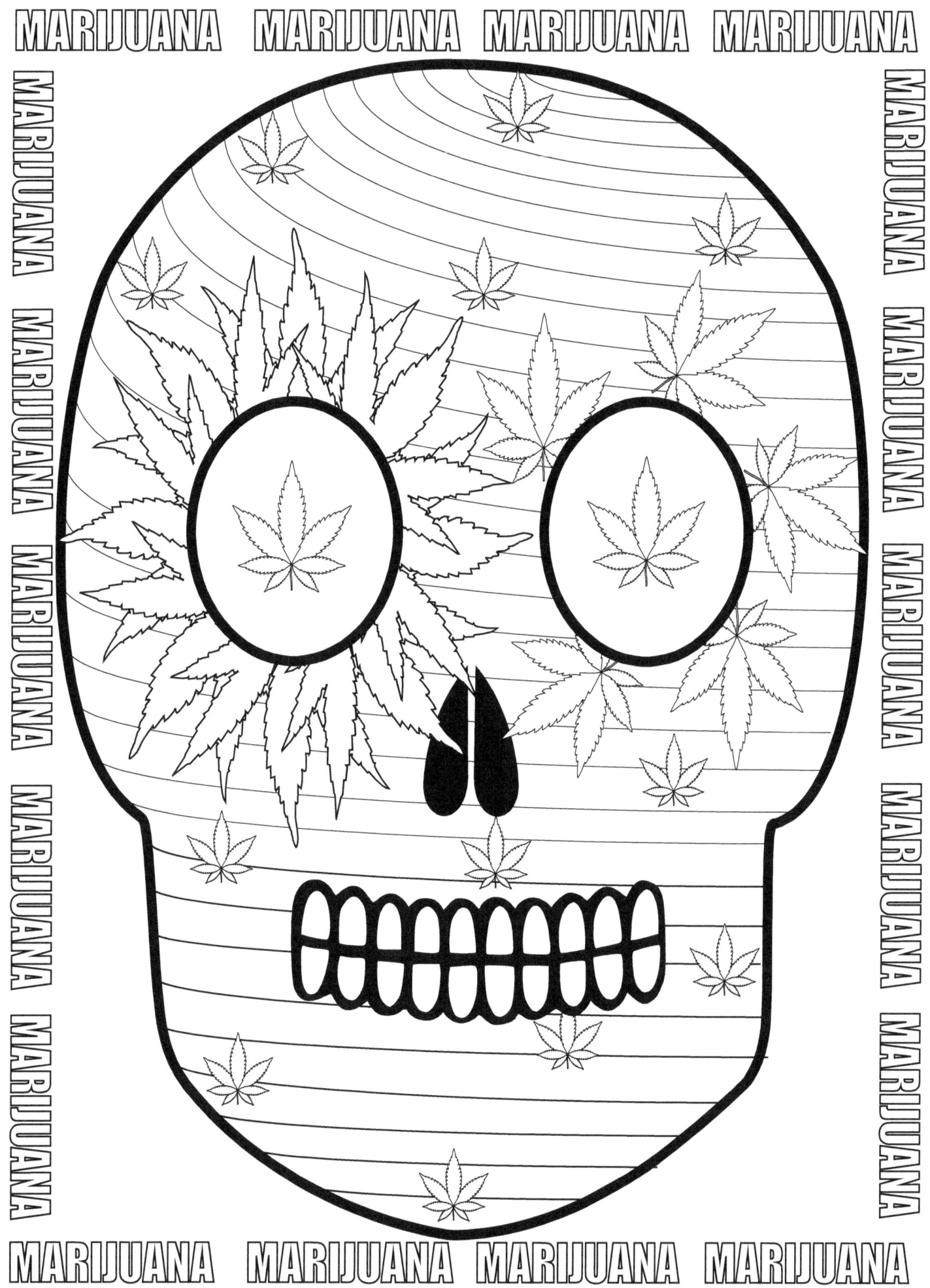

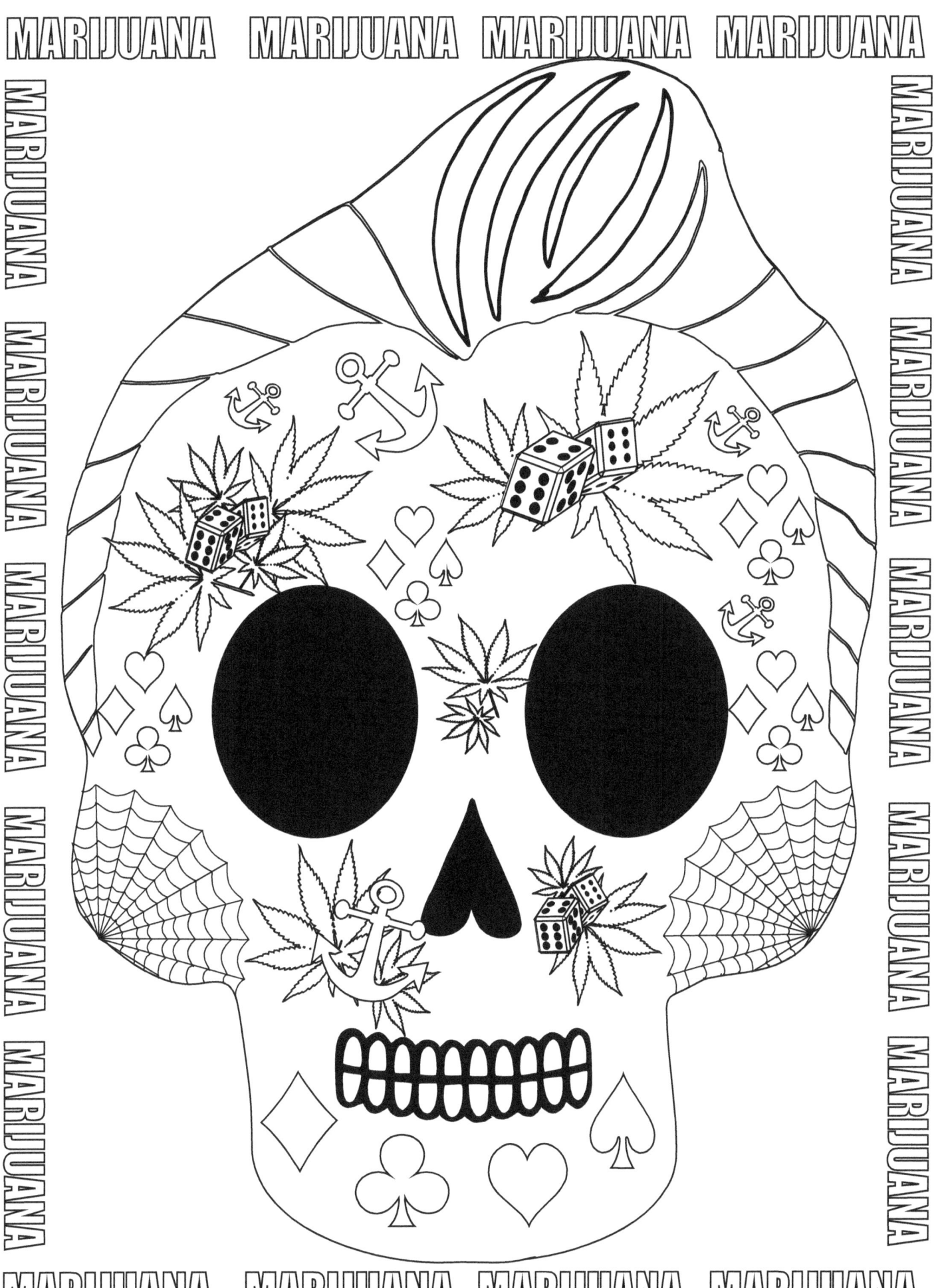

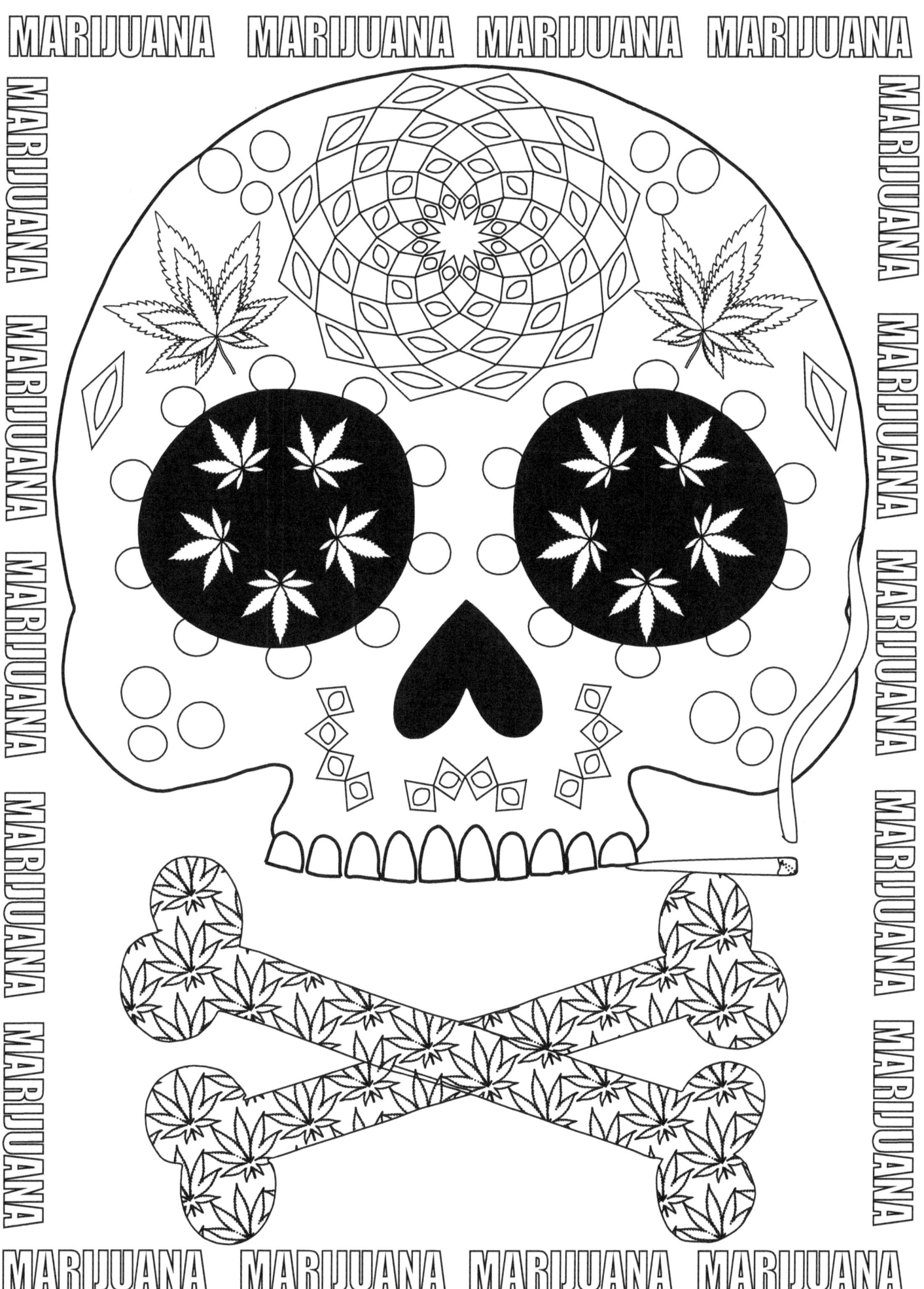

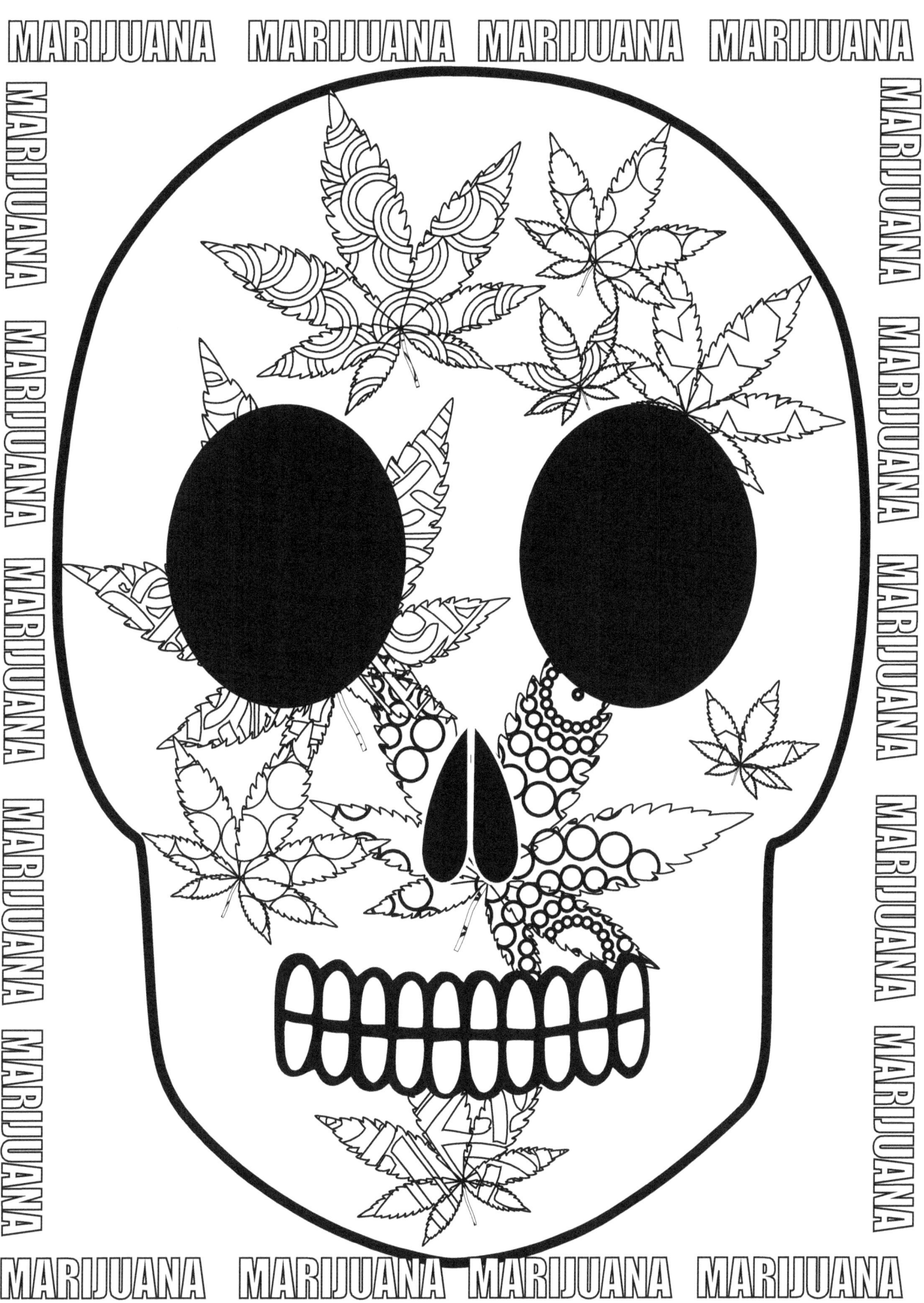

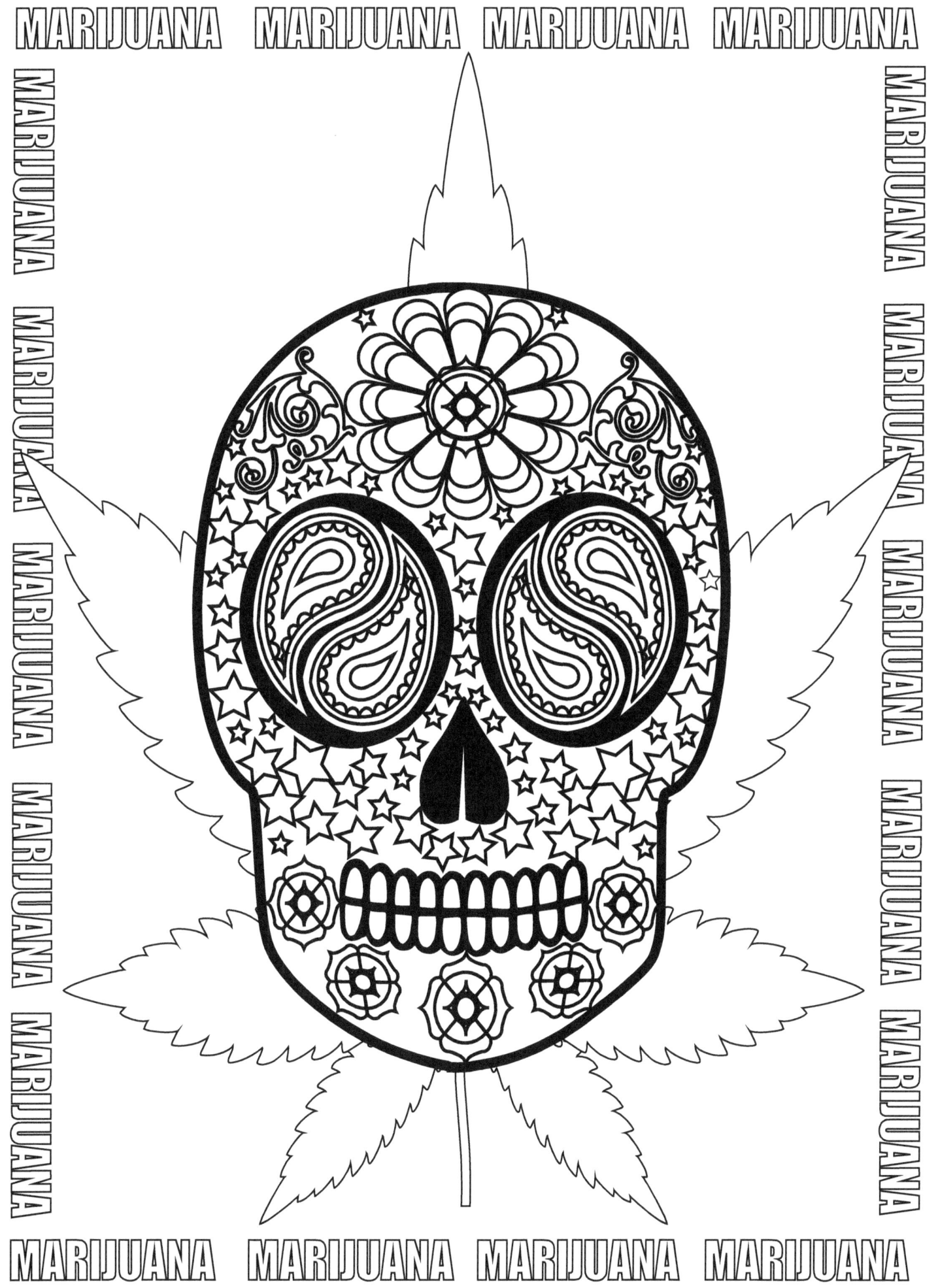

MARIJUANA MARIJUANA MARIJUANA MARIJUANA

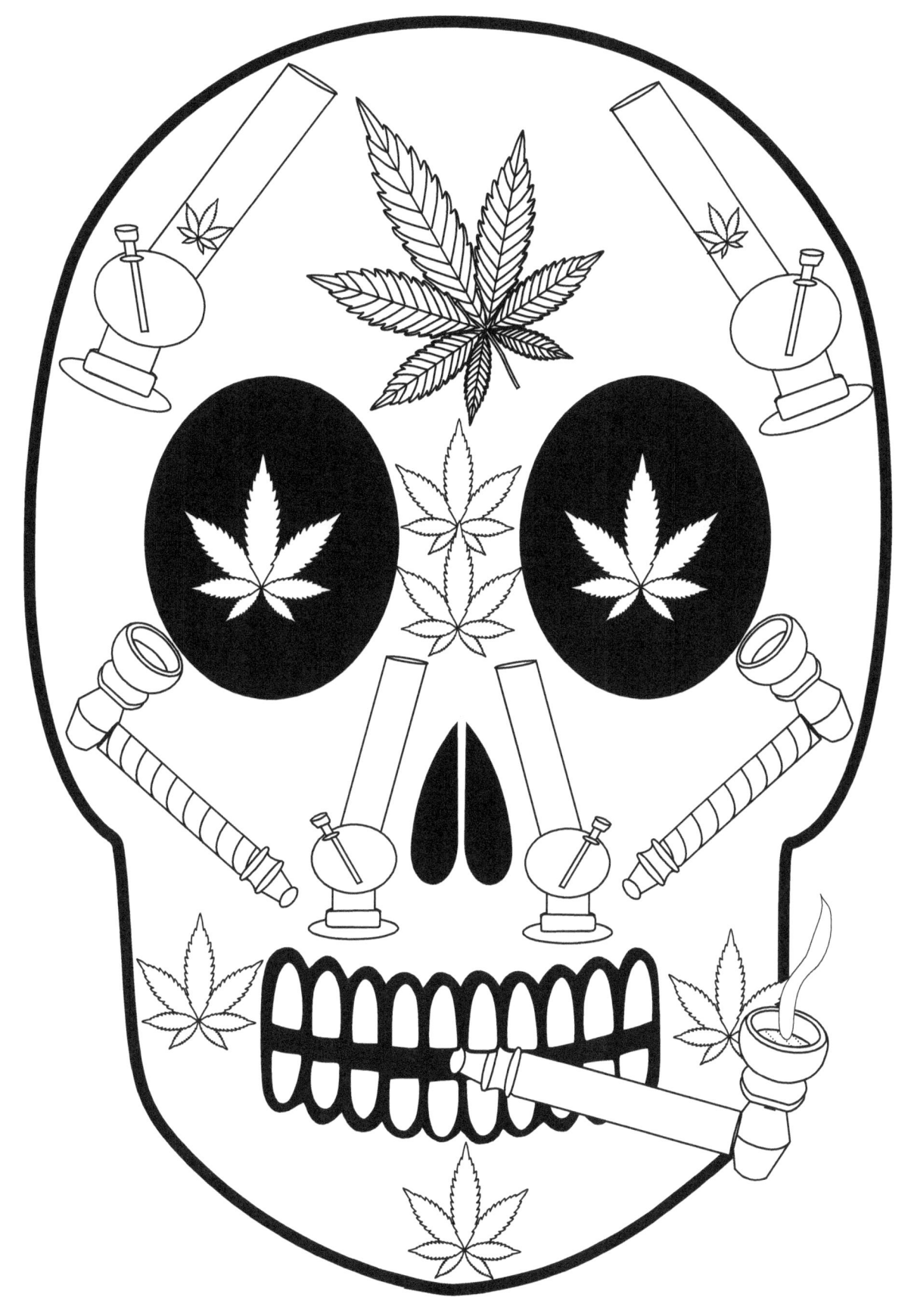

MARIJUANA MARIJUANA MARIJUANA MARIJUANA

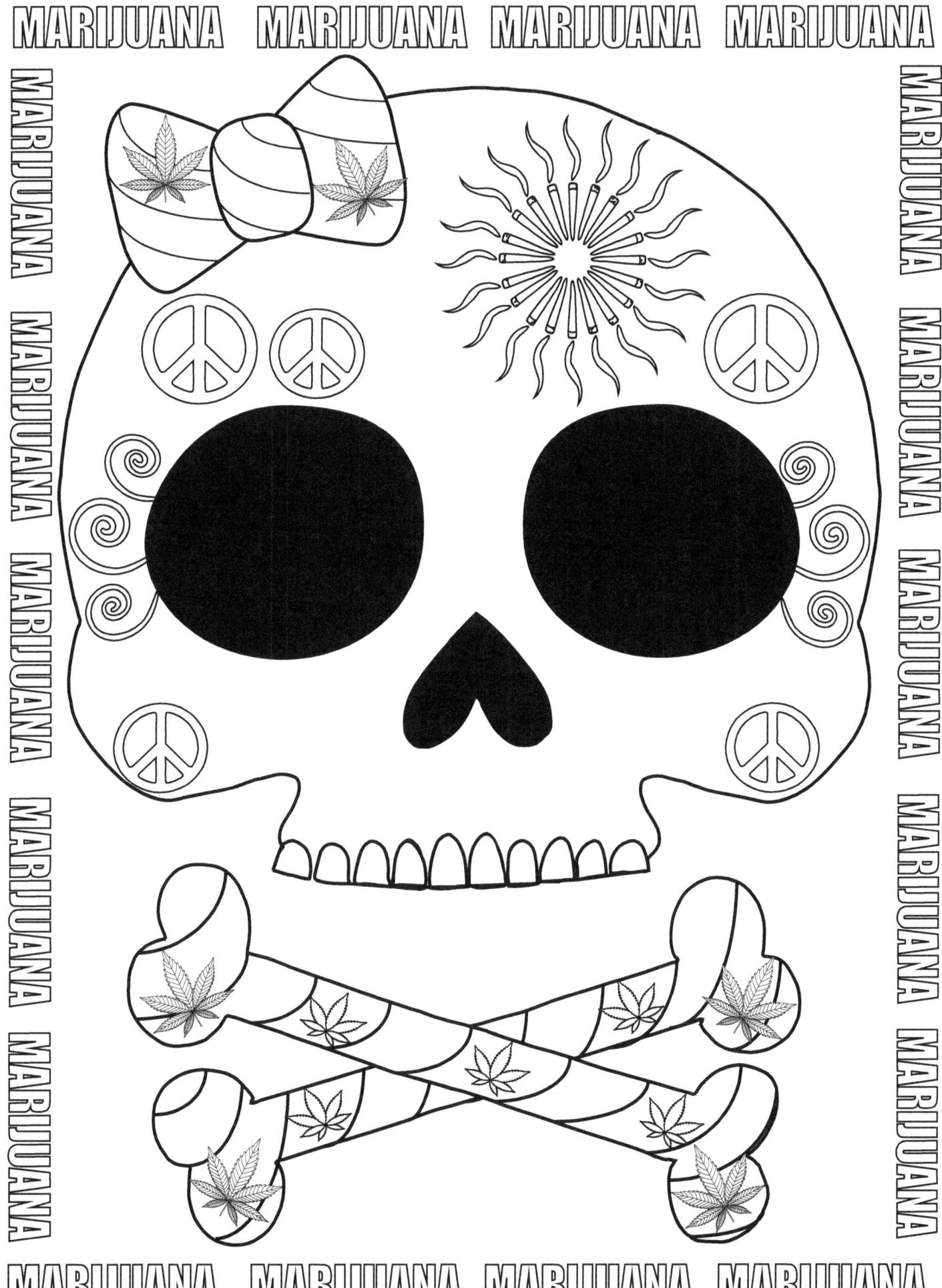

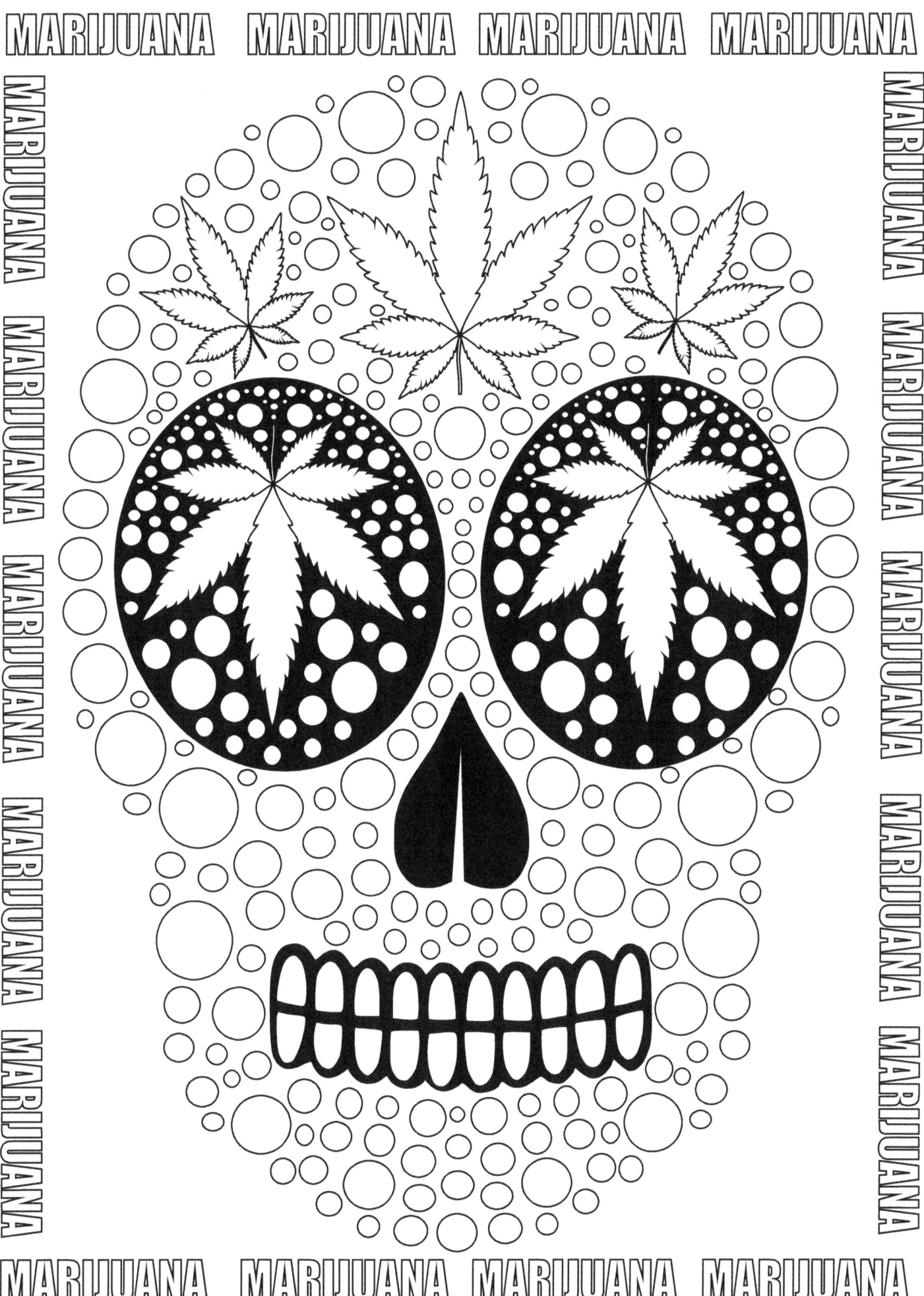

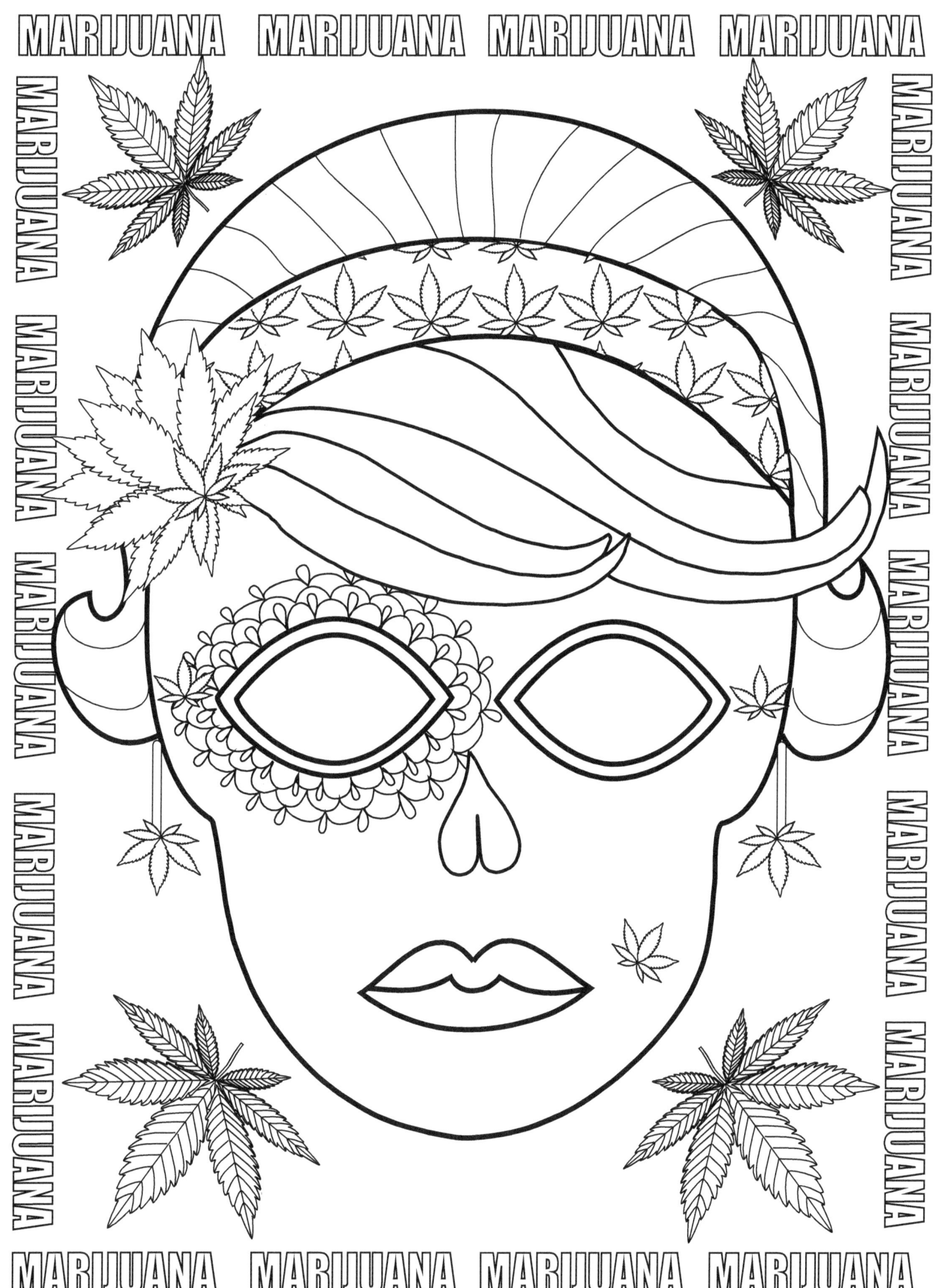

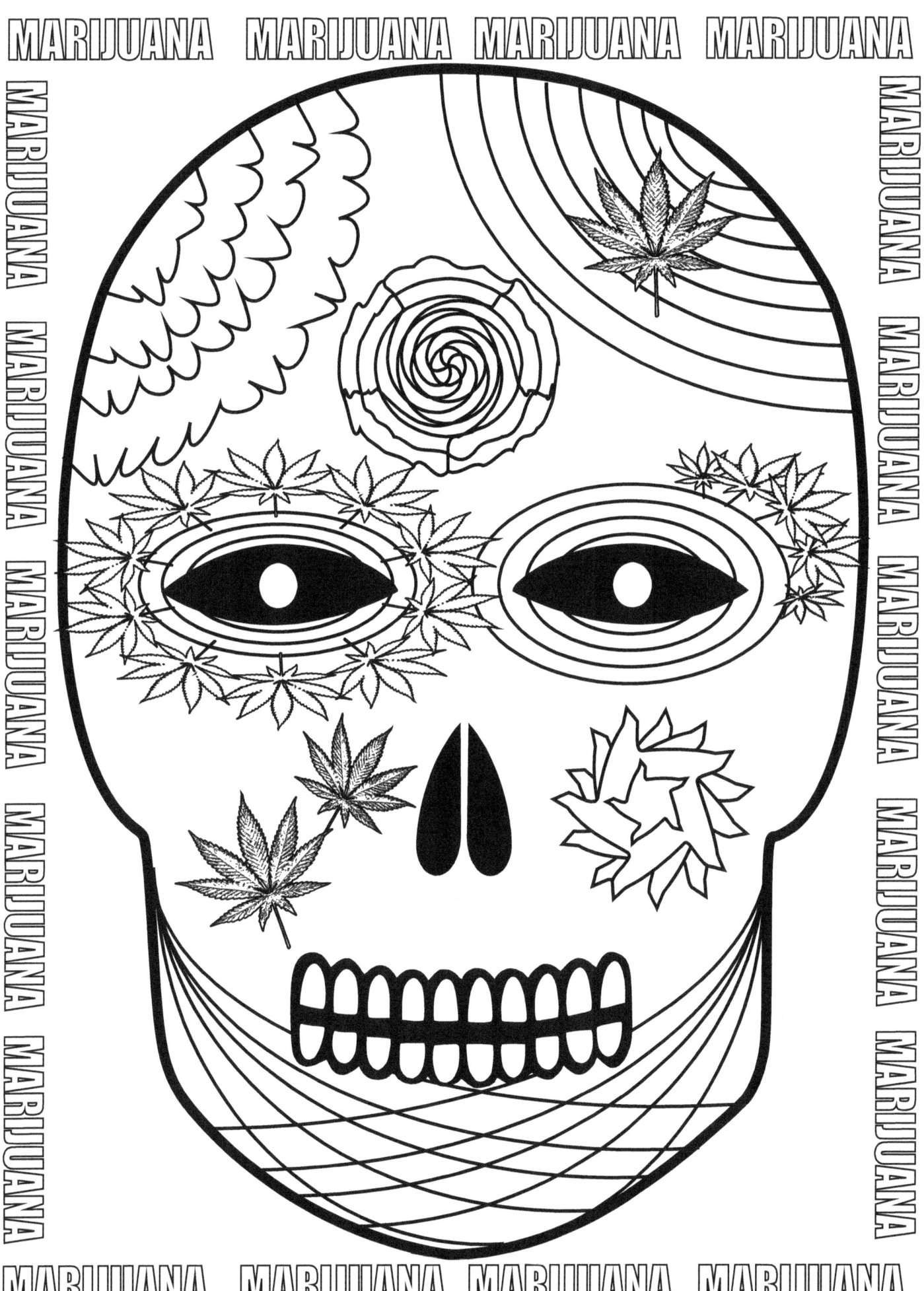

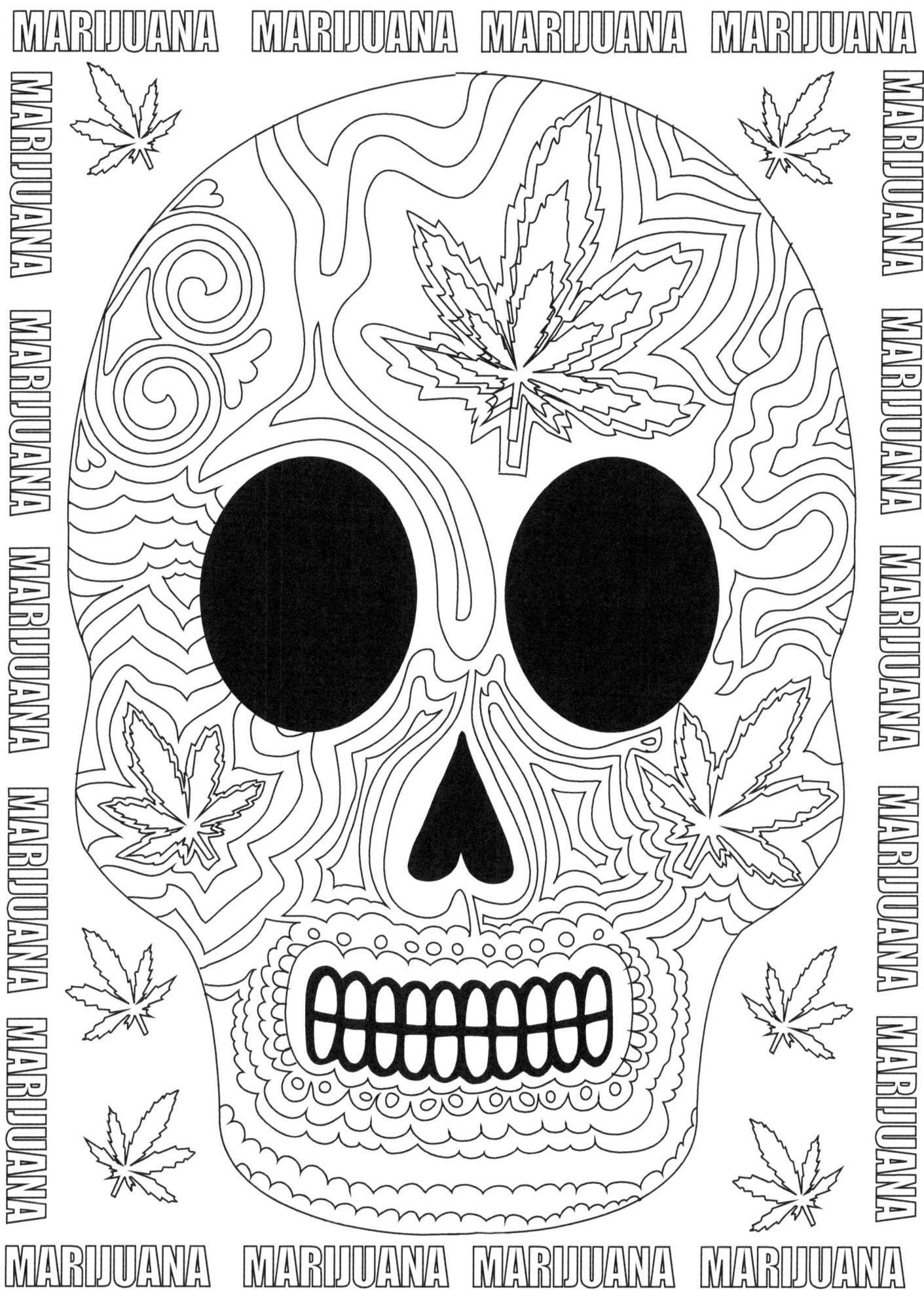

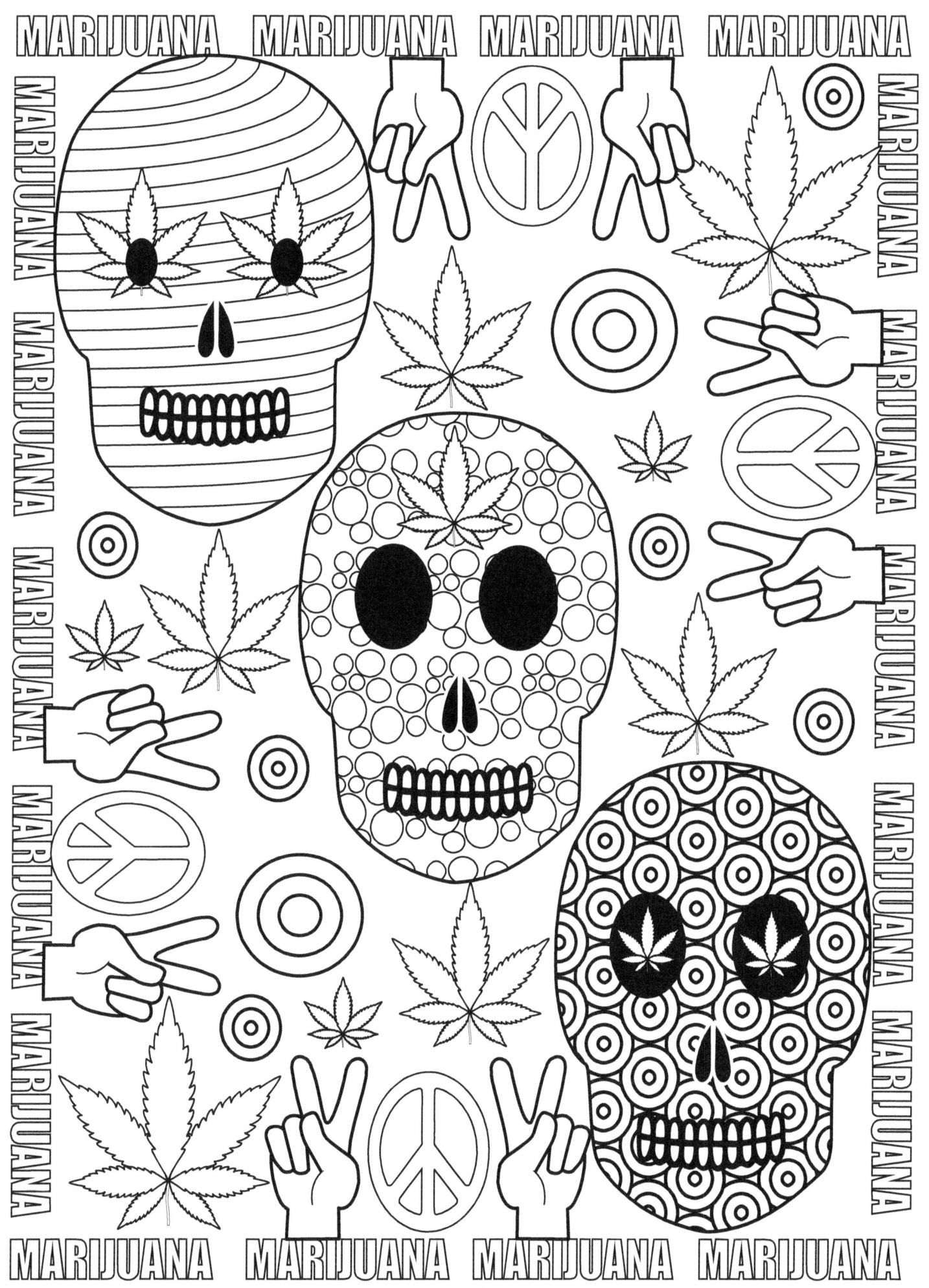

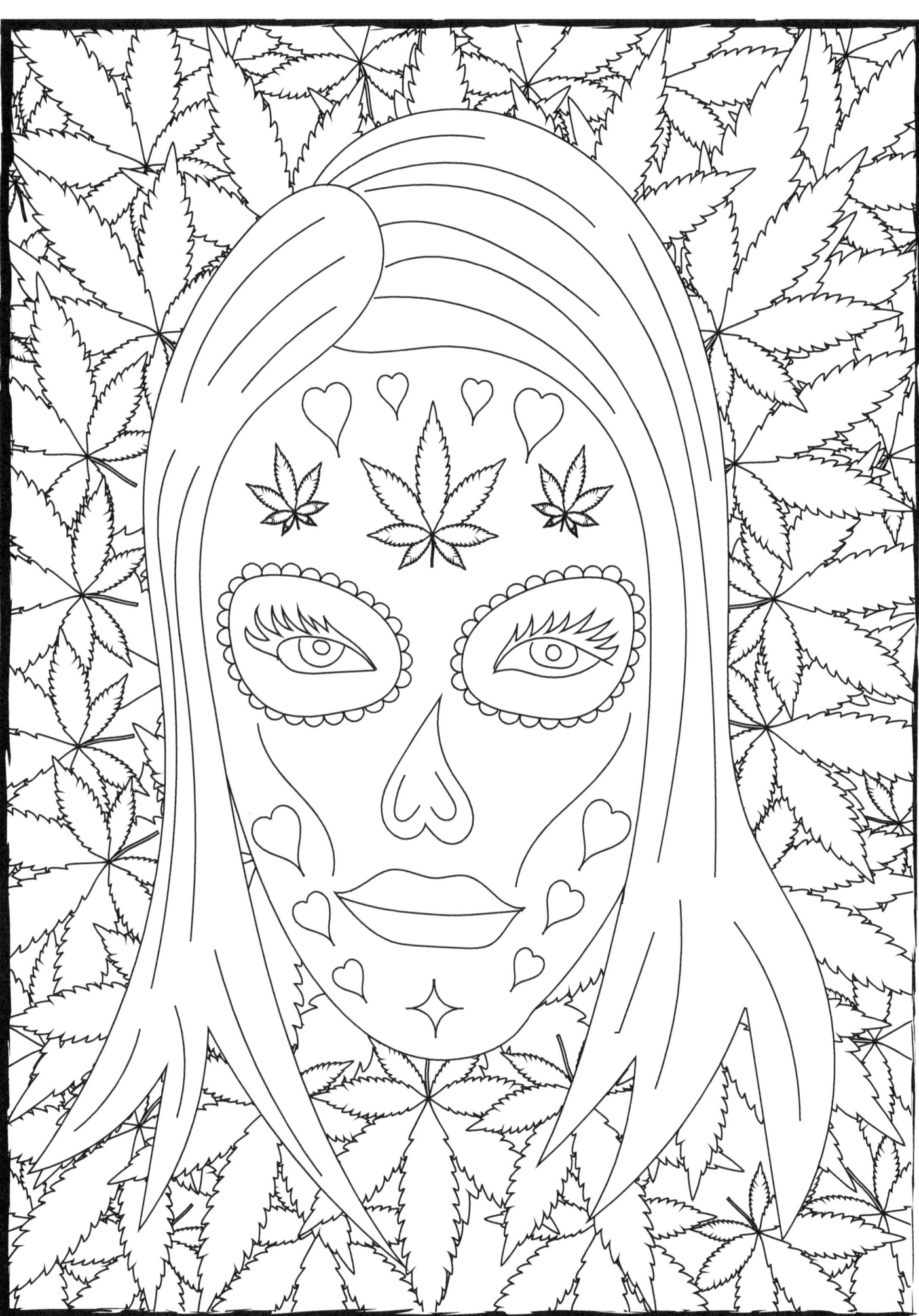

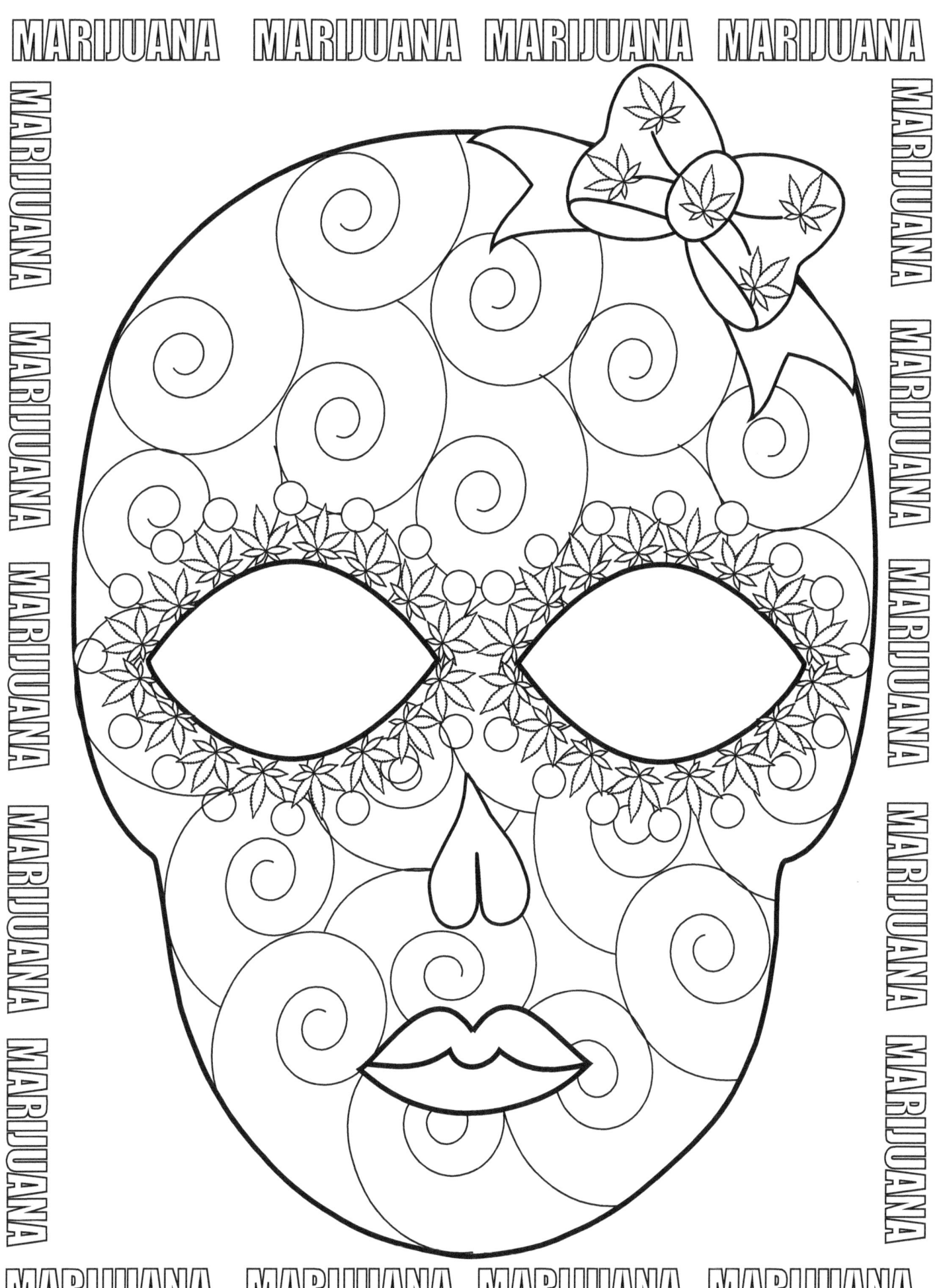

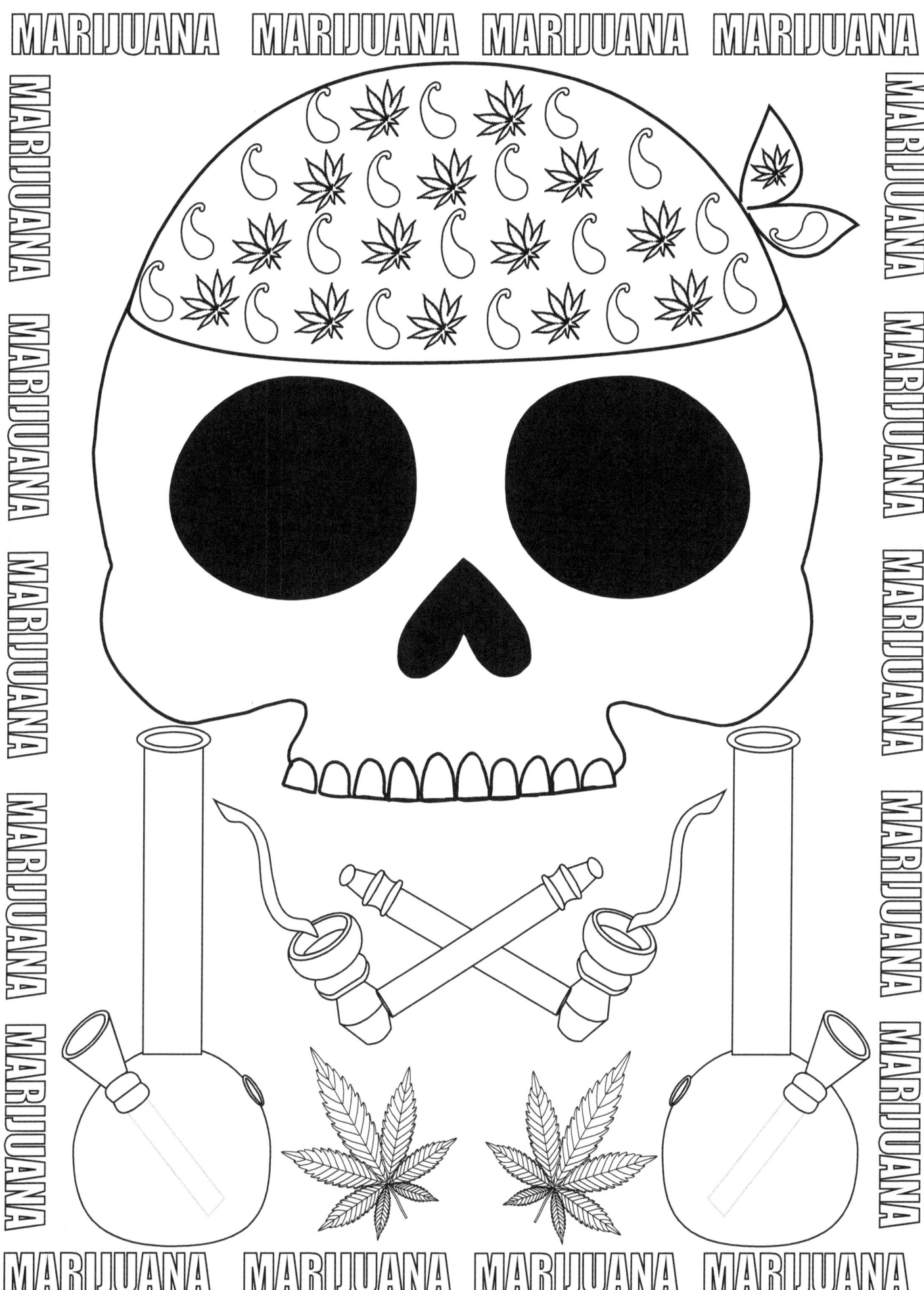

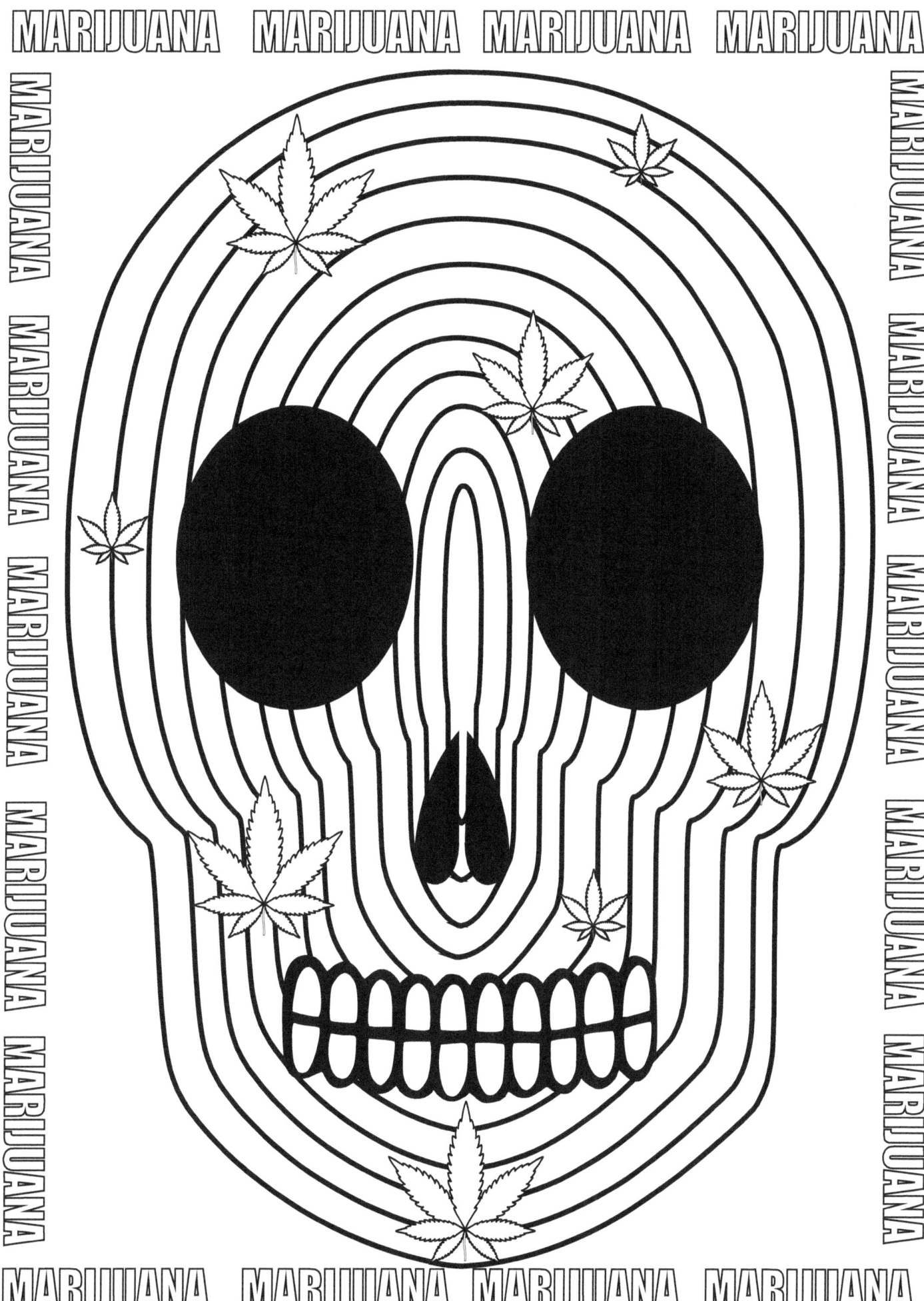

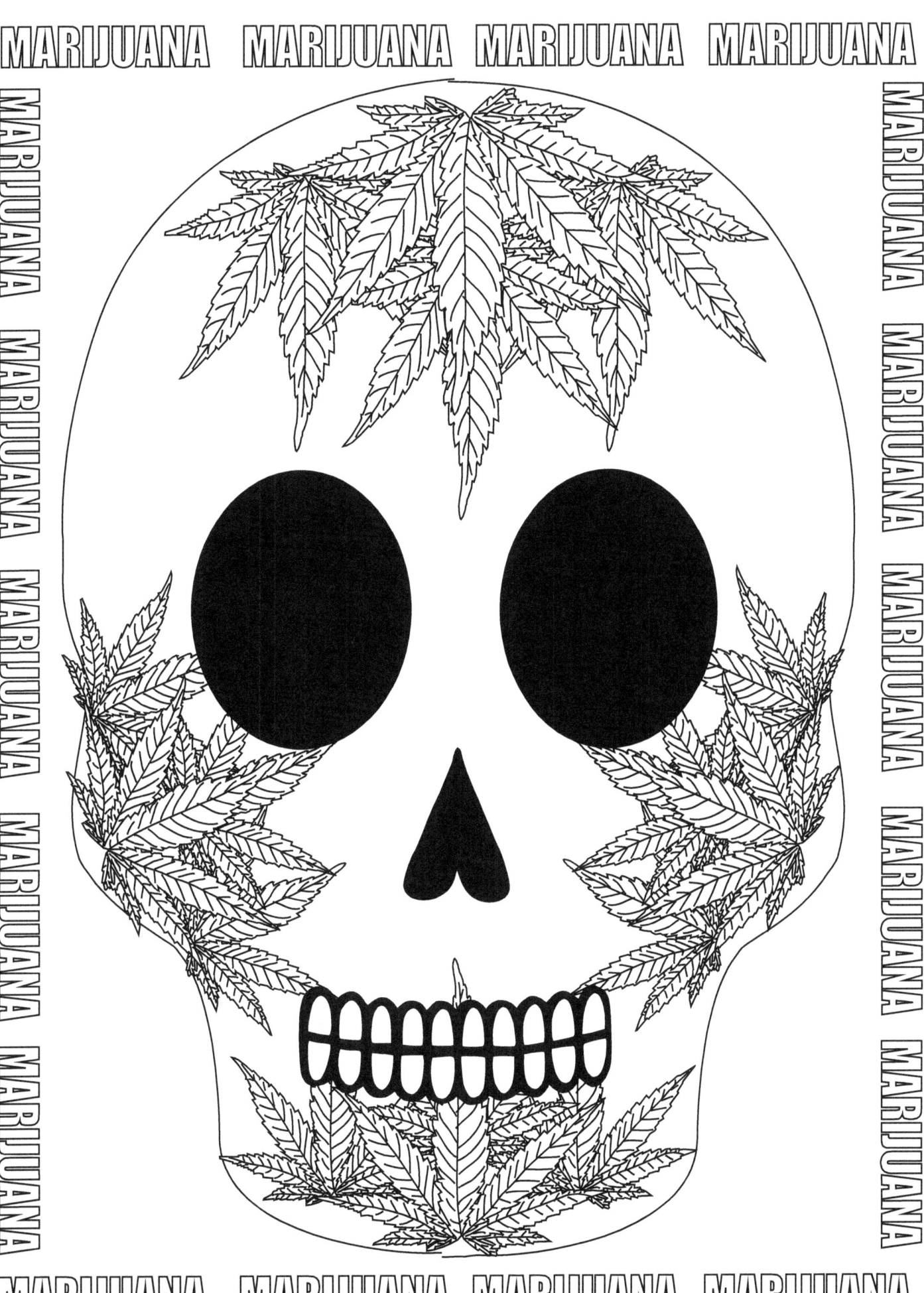

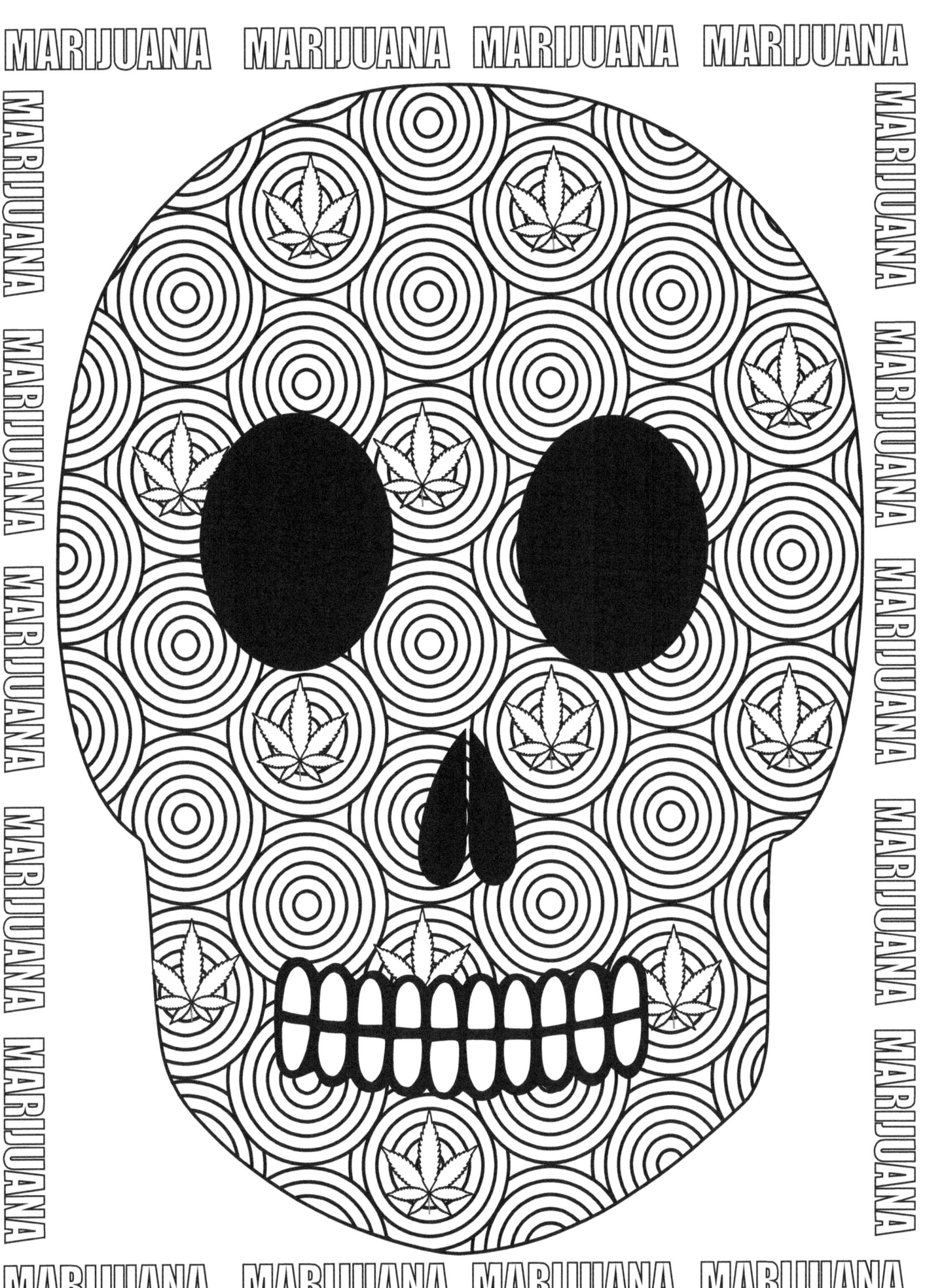

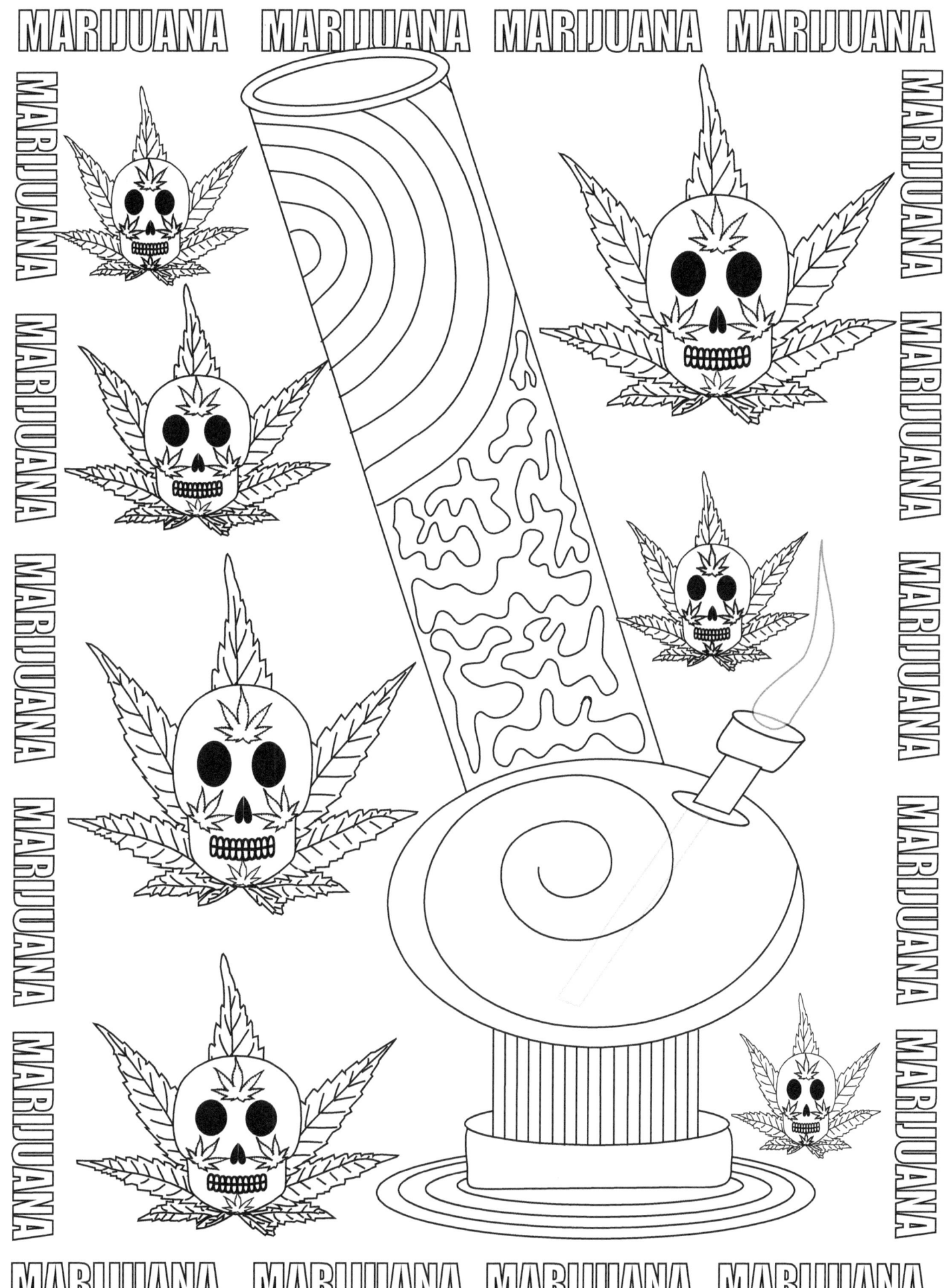

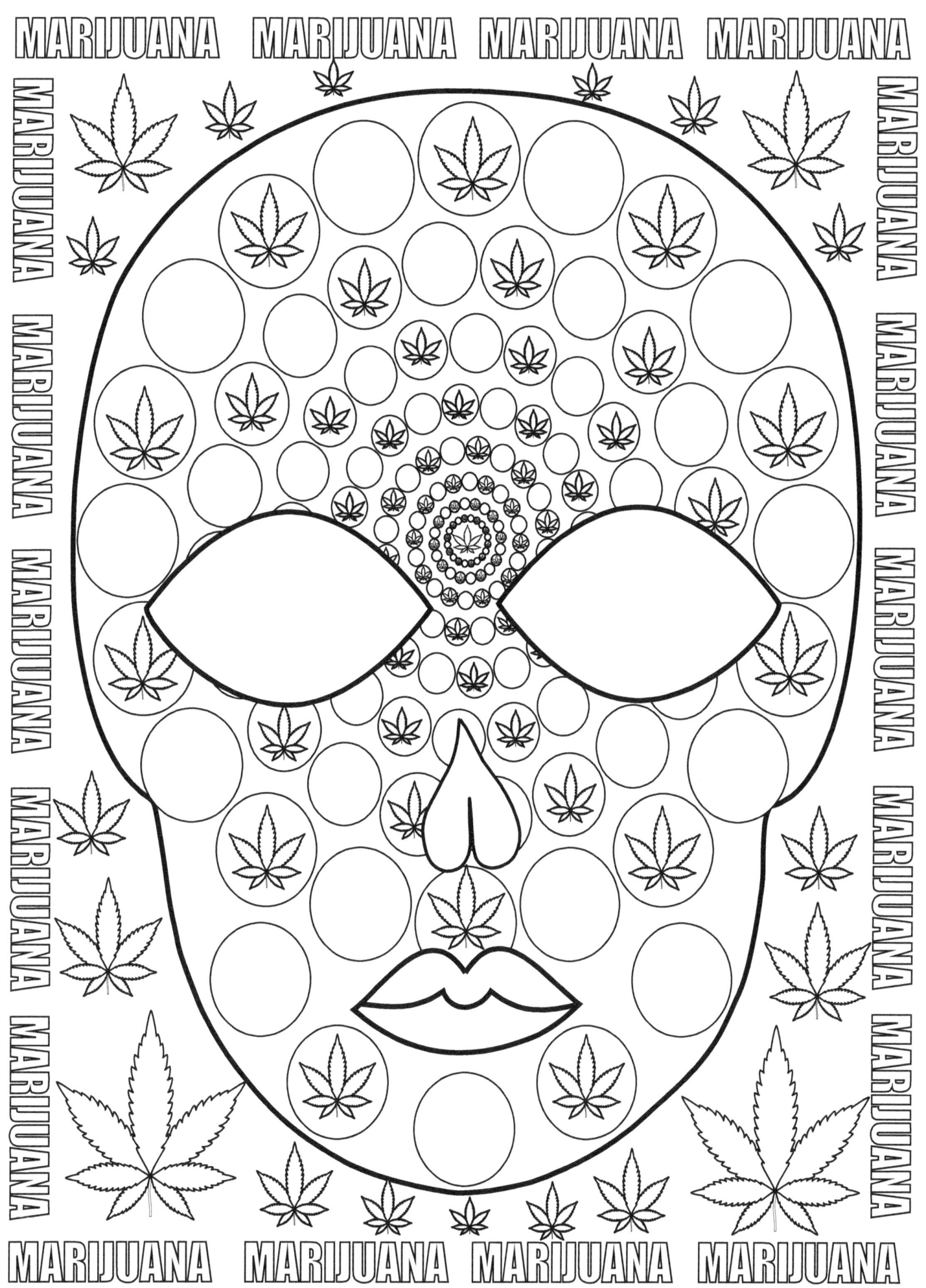

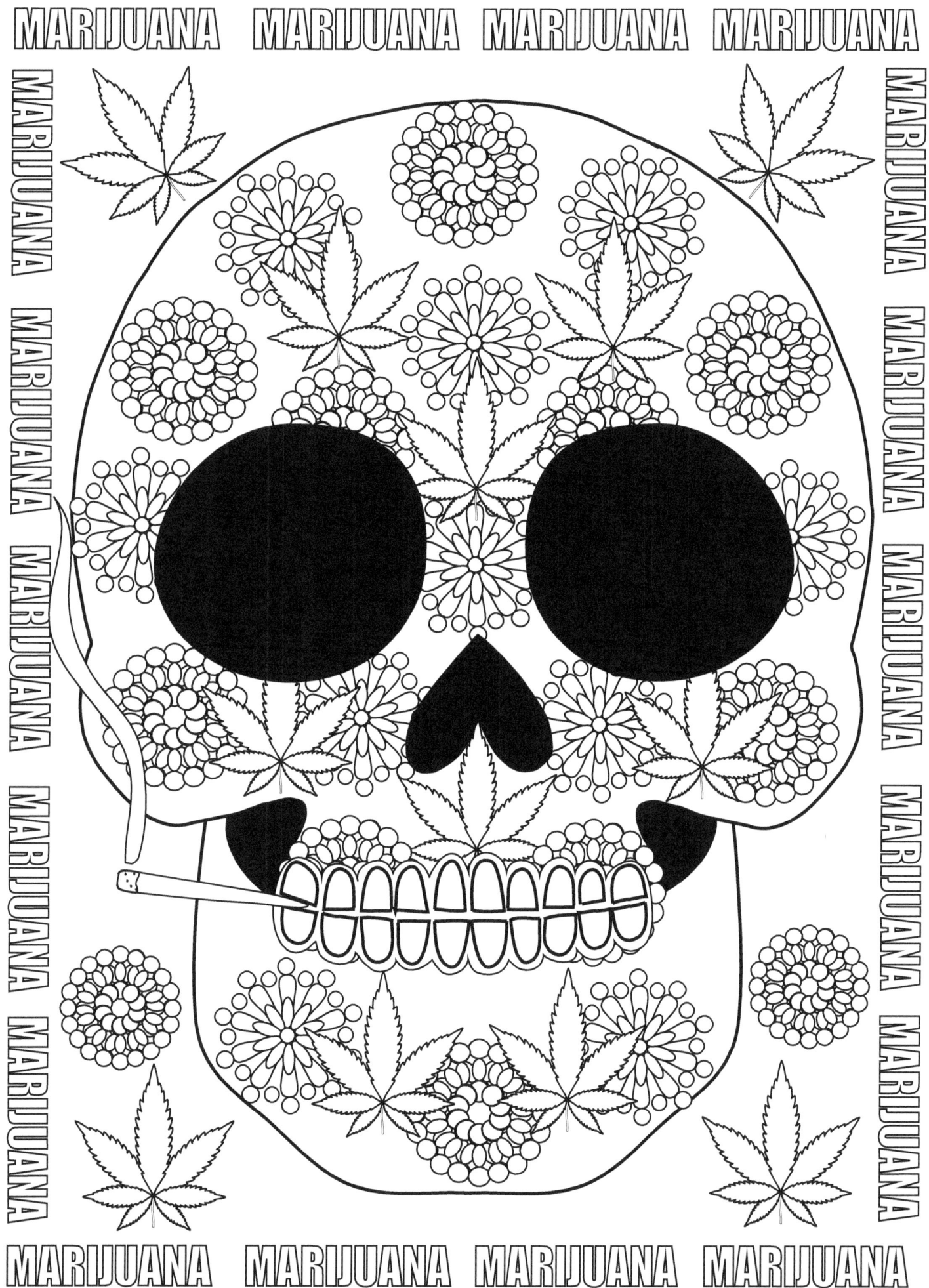

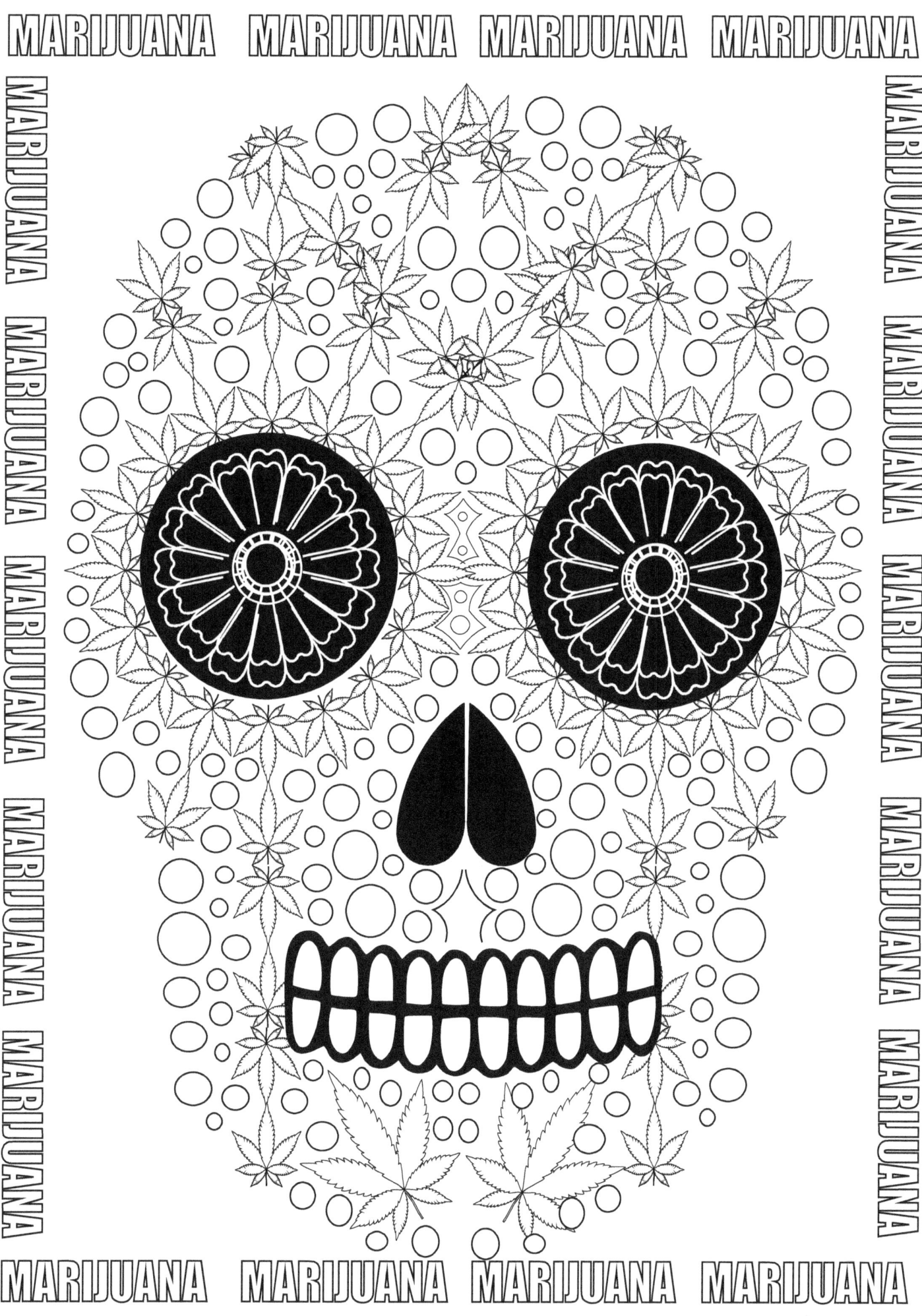

MARIJUANA MARIJUANA MARIJUANA MARIJUANA

MARIJUANA
MARIJUANA
MARIJUANA
MARIJUANA
MARIJUANA
MARIJUANA
MARIJUANA
MARIJUANA

MARIJUANA
MARIJUANA
MARIJUANA
MARIJUANA
MARIJUANA
MARIJUANA
MARIJUANA
MARIJUANA

MARIJUANA MARIJUANA MARIJUANA MARIJUANA

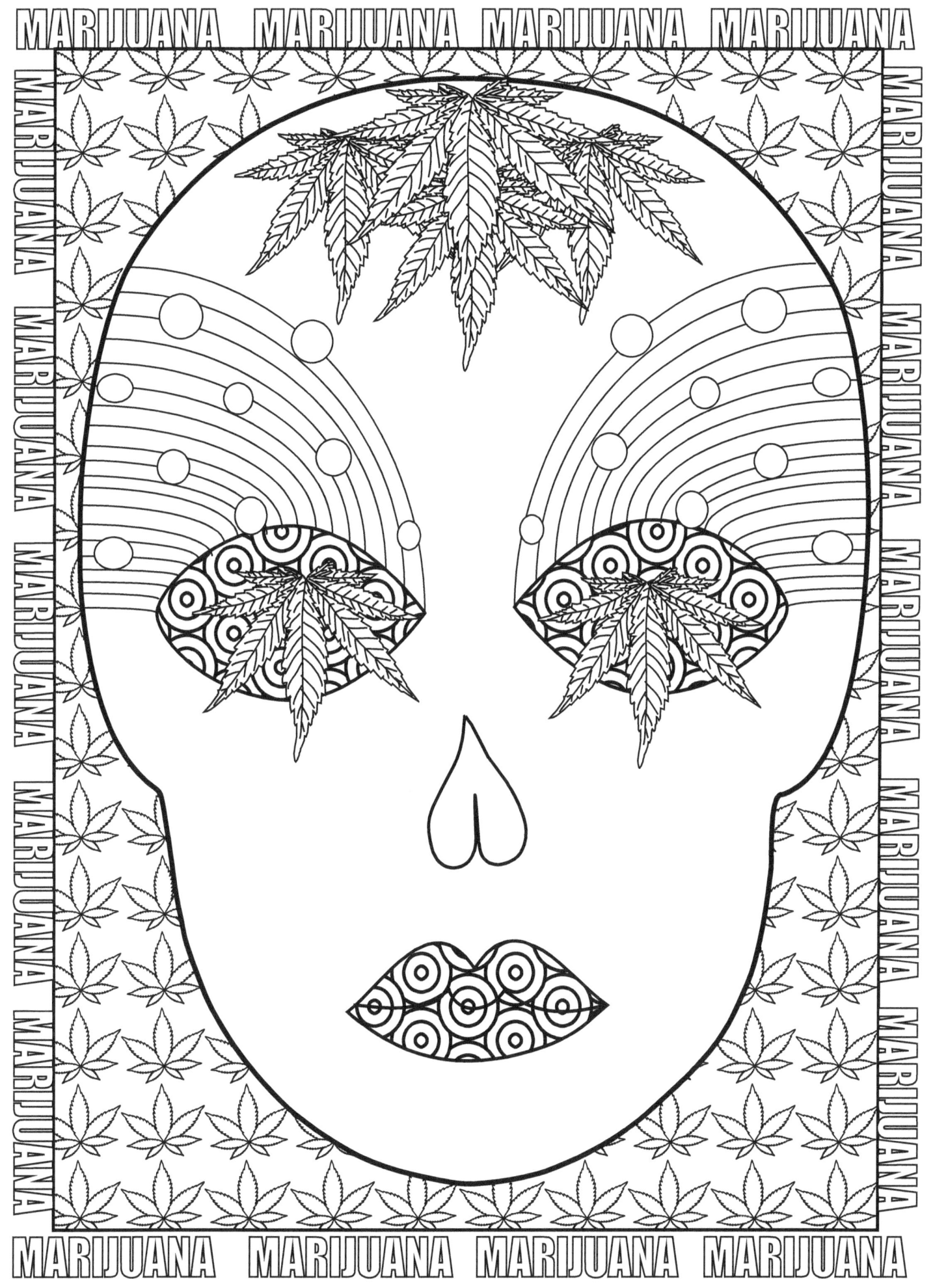

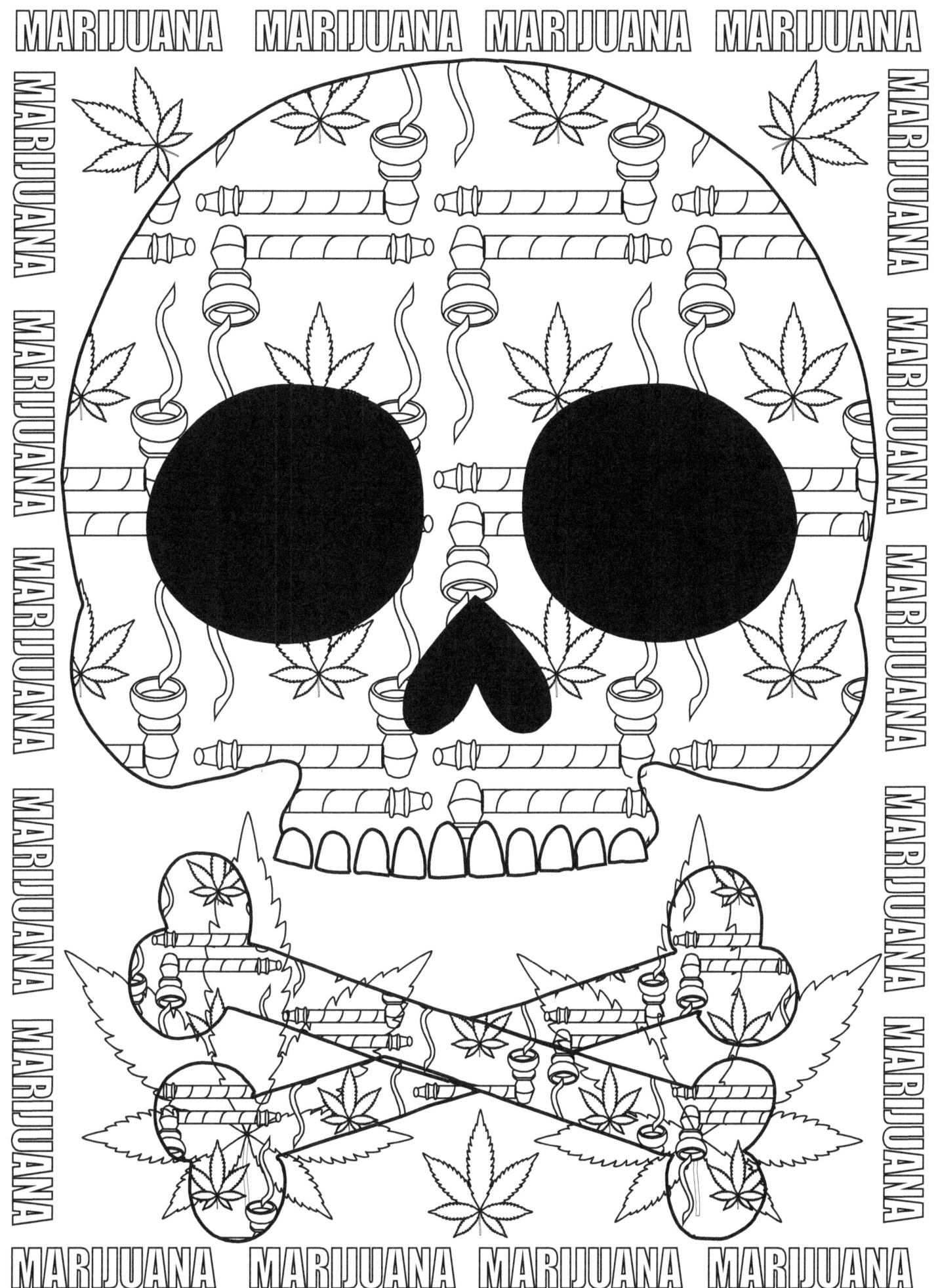

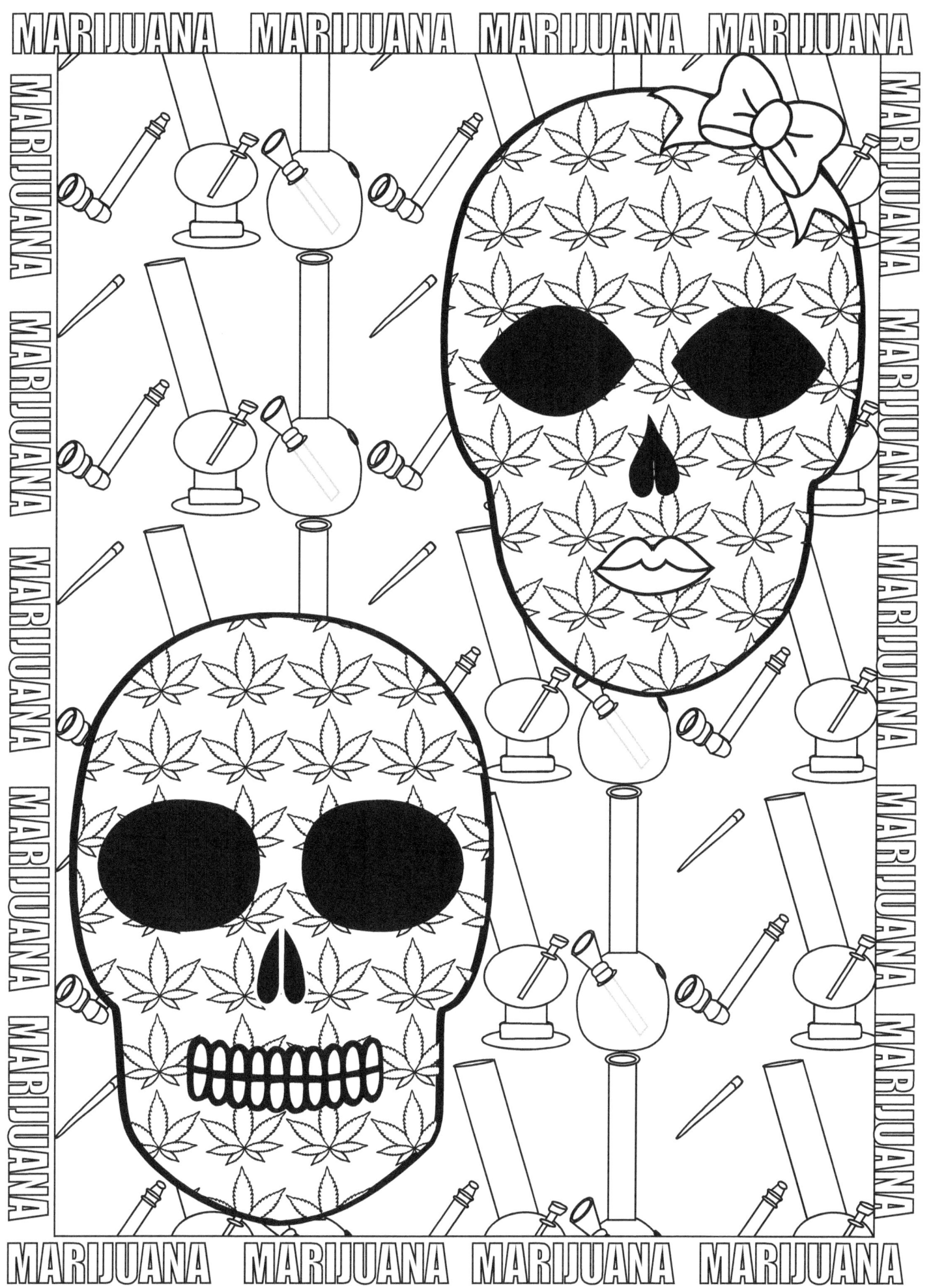

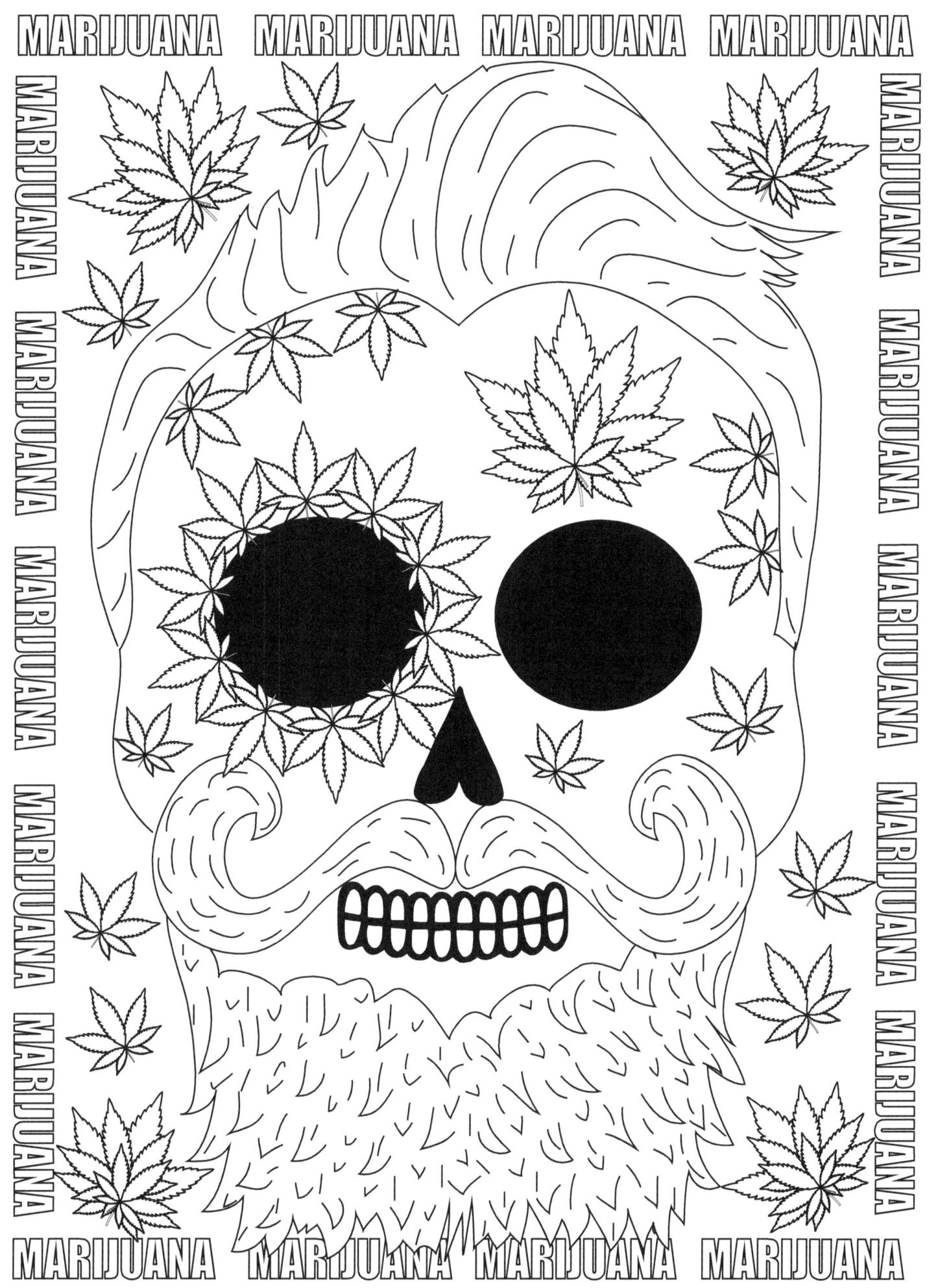

MARIJUANA MARIJUANA MARIJUANA MARIJUANA

MARIJUANA

MARIJUANA

MARIJUANA

MARIJUANA

MARIJUANA

MARIJUANA

MARIJUANA

MARIJUANA MARIJUANA MARIJUANA MARIJUANA

MARIJUANA MARIJUANA MARIJUANA MARIJUANA

MARIJUANA

MARIJUANA

MARIJUANA

MARIJUANA

MARIJUANA

MARIJUANA

MARIJUANA

MARIJUANA

MARIJUANA

MARIJUANA

MARIJUANA

MARIJUANA

MARIJUANA MARIJUANA MARIJUANA MARIJUANA

www.ingramcontent.com/pod-product-compliance
Lightning Source LLC
Chambersburg PA
CBHW080630190526
45169CB00009B/3341